THE RISE OF URBAN AMERICA

ADVISORY EDITOR

Richard C. Wade

PROFESSOR OF AMERICAN HISTORY
UNIVERSITY OF CHICAGO

A BRIEF TREATISE
ON THE POLICE
OF THE
CITY OF NEW YORK

Charles Christian

ARNO PRESS
&
The New York Times

NEW YORK · 1970

Reprint Edition 1970 by Arno Press Inc.

Reprinted from a copy in The University of Chicago Library

LC# 76-112548
ISBN 0-405-02442-8

THE RISE OF URBAN AMERICA
ISBN for complete set 0-405-02430-4

Manufactured in the United States of America

A

BRIEF TREATISE,

ON THE

POLICE

OF THE

CITY OF NEW-YORK.

—◦✣◦—

BY A CITIZEN.

—◦✣◦—

NEW-YORK,

PRINTED BY SOUTHWICK & PELSUE,
No. 3 New, and 68, Vesey-streets,

FOR THE AUTHOR.

—◦✦◦—

1812.

The following brief treatise, on the Police of the City of New-York, is most respectfully addressed to the Honorable the Mayor, and Corporation,

by their Obedient Servant,

THE AUTHOR.

—●❀●—

TREATISE ON THE POLICE.

—

THE population of a large city may be classed under three general heads : Those that are virtuous from choice those that fear the shame attending the detection of crime, and those that are indifferent to shame, and only fear corporeal punishment. The first class, the basis of social order, practices justice without coercion, all that the law has to do with them, is to take care that they are not injured by the others ; the second, composed of persons having, what is termed, a good character, are deterred from the practice of evil by the fear of detection, and the third, made up of those that have been early corrupted by bad example—those whose natural inclination to vice is so ardent as to riumph over good example, and all those that are ruined in reputation by detection, are rendered callous to shame.

The duty of the Police, it would therefore seem, is to guard the first from danger. To endeavour by salutary address, to prevent the second from descending, and to frustrate, or punish the third.

When the population of a city becomes so numerous that the citizens are not all known to each other, then may depredators merge in the mass, and spoliate in secret and safety, and then is the precise time for the organization of a vigilant Police to develope, and frustrate their plans and operations. We have got beyond this point, and it appears to be highly necessary that there should be established, as soon as possible, as complete a system of preventive Police for this city, as our laws will admit of ; with a population increasing beyond all precedent, an immense amount and quick interchange of floating property, and an influx of transient persons, greater than to any city on this side of the Atlantic, it furnishes superior temptations to the cupidity of those sharpers, of all grades, that devote their pernicious talents to the annoyance of society : a brief view of the following branches of this subject, may, in some degree, contribute to the accomplishment of an object of such great public importance.

THIEVES & SHARPERS.
CITY NIGHT WATCH.
STATE PRISON CONVICTS.
PARDONS.
CITY PRISON—BRIDEWELL.
WOMEN OF THE TOWN—PENITENTIARY.
BROTHEL KEEPERS.

GAMBLERS—GAMING HOUSES.

TAVERNS—ARDENT LIQUORS.

PAWN BROKERS—DEALERS IN OLD CLOTHES—
DEALERS IN JUNK AND SHIP IRON.

INTELLIGENCE OFFICES—SERVANTS.

GENERAL OBSERVATIONS—PUBLIC BATHS.

In the class of thieves and sharpers, may be included all those that have been committed and punished for grand and pettit larceny, and come out of prison unreclaimed—thieves yet undetected—all those engaged in passing off counterfeit money—pickpockets, men domesticated in brothels, occasionally the husbands of bawds, as circumstances of fraud or evasion may require, and professed gamblers. This dangerous class of men, that abound in all great cities, and of whom this has an ample proportion, are the standing and peculiar subjects of police vigilance. The precautions they in general observe frequently enable them to elude detection sufficient to warrant their being committed for trial. The only resource then left is to commit them in a summary way, under the act for the punishment of disorderly persons ; which detention affords time, successfully in some instances, to look for evidence to bring them to trial ; but otherwise this punishment, which to the utmost is but sixty days confinement at picking oakum, is very inadequate either to deter or reform its subjects. It fails almost in every instance, as a means of reformation, and, probably, has never been known to discourage, of itself, a hardened offender from returning, as soon as convenient, to his former course of conduct ; yet, as it suspends their career and depredations for sixty days at once, it is, in

that point of view, valuable, and of beneficial operation, though at best but an expedient.

When persons of this description find themselves
locked up for sixty days, the apprehension that sufficient proof will, in the mean time, be found, that may
enable the authority to bring them to trial, renders
them in general very desirous to commute banishment
from the state, or city, for immediate enlargement
from prison, but the magistrates are not authorized to
make such an agreement, yet if a provision of this na-
ture can constitutionally be had, it would have an excellent effect ; under this opinion, I submit the following for consideration : That the mayor, or any two
police magistrates, may be empowered to take, in their
discretion, the voluntary recognizance of a party, so
committed and applying, the breach of which to be
penal, for his, or her, quitting the city as the condition
of enlargement. This, or some other power, should
be vested in the police, to enable them, to harrass, and
compel to absence, those dangerous and incorrigible
characters.

CITY WATCH.

IT is very apparant that a reform is necessary in the
regulation of our night watch, which important branch
of police, is very rarely improved to the perfection it
is susceptible of ; and as I can offer nothing better on
this subject, than that, which has been already proposed, I shall take the liberty to quote that opinion.

" The present manner of posting the night watch
is, in my opinion, and I offer it with great deference,

susceptible of improvement. In stormy weather they are housed in their boxes, when in fact at such time they should be most on the alert, for then the marauder takes advantage of the streets being clear of passengers to accomplish his purpose."

" The following system, I think, furnishes a reasonable expectation that the city would be much more secure under its operation, than that at present in use, especially if connected with a night police, the project of which I submitted in my former communication. I propose that the watch-boxes shall be taken away, and, in their stead, the men furnished with substantial watch-coats, which they shall deposit in the watch-houses when they go off duty. That the sentries, in every part of the city, shall commence duty precisely at the same time, and walk on their posts in the following order :

" For instance, let a sentry be stationed at the corner of Broadway next the Battery, and another at the Park, on the opposite side of the street, the man at the Battery shall walk to the Park, and the sentry at the Park shall walk to the Battery, passing each other at the centre of their station, and so continue during their tour. When crossing the intersecting streets, they shall look down those streets, which caution shall be observed by the sentries in those streets when they cross the corners of Broadway. They would thus have the whole of this post always in view, and every resident therein would be certain that a watchman would pass his door about every third minute.

" I would in this way have the whole city watch in constant activity, subject, also, to such subordinate regulations as the superintending magistrates might judge necessary to keep them vigilant, and the respective posts of such an extent as circumstances may require "

This system is, in all probability, the most perfect that can be practiced, and it may not be too much to say, that it would effectually prevent shop lifting—house-breaking—street-robbery, and nightly depredations on shipping at the wharfs. The constant march, and countermarch of a competent number of able bodied, and faithful men, would furnish a much greater certainty of the safety of persons and property, during the night, than the present practice does, or can afford.

STATE PRISON CONVICTS.

THIS excellent institution, and great receptacle for all convicts in the state, between the highest and low est grades of criminals, discharges its tenants on this city, a great proportion of whom are, it is hoped, penitent, and determined to live, in future, honestly; whilst others, and there is reason to fear not a few, return on society unreclaimed.

It is not necessary to enter into a detail of the temptations which this city present, for a floating residence, to the discharged convict, who, with a ruined character, sees every individual in the county he was sent from on their guard against him, for these, no doubt, will readily occur to every person that reflects on the subject, and that the discharge in this city, of the state prison convicts is, productive of bad consequences to its inhabitants; of this I am fully certain, nor should I make the assertion, if I had not positive knowledge of the fact.

It is a serious matter to this city, if it shall continue, thus to receive so great an accession of vice superadded to its own located depravity, and when the rapid increase of the population of this great state, and the consequent accumulation of vice (unless the character of man should undergo a sudden and beneficial change) are considered, the pernicious effects must, it is to be feared, ultimately be immense.

There are two just and practicable means for reducing this evil to an indispensable ratio, viz. The Legislature to direct, that the State Prison establishment shall be removed as near to the center of the state as may be convenient to internal navigation. In this way the inconvenience would be equalized, as nearly as possible, on all parts of the state, or, if it is indispensable for the convenience of manufactures, safety, or otherwise, to continue it where it is, the prisoners, as enlarged, may be conducted to the respective county prisons from whence they were sent, and there discharged at the expence of their county, or of the state. The first plan, however, appears to be the most eligible, it is certainly equitable, and it would seem that no cogent objection can be urged against it.

PARDONS.

THE righteous tenacity of the law in defence of individual as well as public liberty—the characteristic humanity of our courts and juries—the great reluctance of grand inquests to indict, as long as reasonable hopes of reform may be entertained—the avidity with which every circumstance in' favour of a prisoner is seized on by the traverse jury, and the absolute necessity of full, free, and clear evidence to establish guilt to conviction, renders it almost a matter of certainty that no prisoner is taken from the bar to punishment unjustly. After all those fences and precautions, justice relenting, and mourning, over the fate of the offender, shows him mercy personified in the chief magistrate of the state, and encourages him with hopes of pardon for his crimes. Such is the merciful character of our jurisprudence, and may it ever so continue, but, though every humane· man ought and does, when solicited, lend his influence to obtain the pardon of proper subjects of mercy, it is to be regretted that they have not, always, sufficient resolution to resist similar applications from hardened· offenders. The executive has, in general, no knowledge of the applicants for pardon, but what he derives from the court that tried them, and the citizens of the vicinity, and their recommendation is usually successful. How cautious then should they be, not to permit their humanity and feelings to be in fluenced by specious appearances, and the arts of those, whose lives are devoted to stratagem and deceit, for there can be no doubt, when the apparant repentance is not sincere, that a pardon returns on society an offender more hardened, and more mischievously qualified to annoy society than when· he was committed. The numerous instances of pardoned convicts having abused the mercy of government, fully justify these remarks.

When application is made for the pardon of a criminal from this city, whose previous character is not well known to the governor or judges, it might be profitable to refer for information, on those points, to the committing justice, who, of course, has examined minutely into those particulars, and must be acquaint. ed with a number of facts, fully demonstrative of the character of the applicant, which are not brought before the court, and in all cases, where the person to be par. doned has had associates in his crimes, full and candid information of them, their haunts, and practices, given to the police, should be an indispensable condition of pardon, by this precaution much important information may be obtained for the prevention of crimes, and the apprehension of the informant himself, should he return to his former bad practices, rendered more certain.

CITY PRISON. BRIDEWELL.

THE defects of this establishment are so obvious, that I shall pass them over in silence, and proceed at once, to a statement of such improvements as are necessary and practicable, and may be applied to it.

It is proposed that a small, neat, and commodious prison shall be erected in the rear of, or somewhere near, the new City-Hall, for the safe keeping, till trial, of persons accused. It is not necessary to have this a large building, as our criminal courts are now held every month, probably one (considering the great num. ber of persons that are admitted to bail) large enough to contain a hundred persons, would be sufficiently ca. pacious until the city becomes so extensive as to ren. der an increase of courts and prisons indispensable.

The present City Prison would answer, though a situation retired, and out of view of that elegant part of the city, would be more suitable for a prison ; nor does the appearance of that edifice correspond with the majestic architecture of the new City.Hall.

It is necessary for the convenience of the public authorities—of prisoners obtaining counsel and bail, and for bringing those to trial who cannot procure, or be admitted to bail, that this prison should be near the courts, and consonant to the humane maxim of the law, that, " the accused is presumed to be innocent until found guilty by his jury;" no further coercion should be used than what may be necessary for safe keeping, good order, and the most perfect cleanliness.

This building should be laid out into several apartments for the purpose of classing, in the discretion of the committing magistrates, the prisoners as committed, and a large yard attached, in which, under secure regulations, they may be permitted to walk, and take air.   There should be a bath and wash room, to which prisoners ought, in the first instance, to be taken, and made to cleanse themselves thoroughly, and, when not provided with a change of clean linen and clothes, be supplied by the public with suitable apparel until their own can be washed, and immediately before being conducted to trial, they should be made to bathe, and have their clothes ready clean to put on.

There would be no public expence attending this system of cleaning, for the prisoners should wash their own clothes, or pay for having it done, and the bath could be heated, when the season would render it necessary, from the kitchen fire by ordinary mechanical arrangement in erecting the building. The prison should be visited once a week by a committee of the common council, and no relaxation of cleanliness permitted.

It may be fairly presumed that under such a system, no inconvenience could arise from having the city prison erected on the site proposed, especially when considered that it would be evacuated, or nearly so, every month ; on the other hand, there can be no doubt, that it would be highly inconvenient for the public business, and to the prisoners generally, to have it remote from the courts ; there is nothing can counterbalance this consideration but that of health, which, doubtless, may be preserved amongst a small number, in the midst of the city, by due attention to cleanliness.

It is proposed that this prison (which for distinction sake, and being appropriate, may be called the City-Prison) should be separate from the prison designed for punishment, for these reasons, namely, The City-Prison proposed, is to keep persons in safe custody, only, until their trials are had. It is necessary, on the part of the public, that the accused should be convenient to the magistrates for examination and trial, and highly so, for the accused, that they should (before trial) be convenient to their counsel and friends. But none of these circumstances are applicable to the prison for punishment after trial, and it may, therefore, with great advantage to all parties, be removed from the center of the city. Under this opinion, I submit the propriety of erecting a new prison to be denominated Bridewell, or, House of Correction, in the vicinity of the new Alms house, and that its economy shall be founded on the penitentiary system of punishment.

Of all the means used for reforming convicts, probably none can be so effectual as solitary confinement. It not only invites, but it forces reflection on the most inert and depraved mind, and without at all partaking of cruelty, is a formidable punishment.

"An act for erecting in the city of New-York, a prison for solitary confinement," passed 30th March, 1802, authorizes the corporation to erect such a prison. The efficacy of solitary confinement has been fully experienced in the State-Prison; it breaks down and tames the most refractory spirits, and although little sentiment may be expected from bridewell convicts, yet the national characteristic (love of liberty) will retain its influence, and be felt, by the most vicious, till the last pulse of life, and reformation, which ordinary punishment cannot induce, nor force, may be accomplished by the reflection and terrors of solitary imprisonment.

There can be no doubt, but that punishment should be tempered to character, and, consequently, that with us, solitary confinement for petit larceny, and other crimes, would, in many instances, produce a penitent effect, and may be adopted to great advantage in this prison, but, on no pretence should the keepers be permitted to exercise this authority, nor to put a prisoner under any other restraint, or discipline, than that which may be set forth in his sentence, unless for attempt to break prison, or for violence that no other way can be restrained; and when such an occasion would occur, report thereof should immediately be made to the visiting committee for their investigation and decision.*

* The life of Baron Trenk fully exemplifies the effect of solitary confinement on men of the greatest fortitude of mind.

The prisoners may be employed to great advantage, under proper economy and discipline, at the following work:

Making Cut Nails.

Sawing Stone.

Polishing Marble.

Picking Oakum.

Chopping Rags.

Sticking Cards,

and such other employment as may be immediately practiced without inconvenience or waste. The strictest order should be established, and the most rigid system of cleanliness enforced, from which no relaxation should be permitted, for persons accustomed to wallow in filth, and drunkenness, labour under constant hydrophobia, and will, if possible, avoid the application of soap and water.

The classification of the prisoners should, as much as possible, be in proportion to their respective grade of crimes; this being, though not always, the best public criterion of depravity, and as few of them permitted to associate together as the convenience of labour may permit, for jollity and indifference to situation and events, are always the companions of a numerous association of such persons, when not under the eye of a task master, and the obscene conversations that are frequently had, the stratagems speculated on by old offenders, tend to the greater corruption of those convicts not hackneyed in criminal address.

The cleansing of the prison and prisoners, should be systematized under the orders of the board of health, and a committee of the common council inspect the prison once every week.

WOMEN OF THE TOWN.

AN impartial examination of the miserable condition of those unhappy women, at once the victims and outcasts of society, might make even a stoic doubt, whether most to pity or condemn; in general, seduced, and basely abandoned to ruin by miscreants that escape with impunity, or for a petty fine, the price of the vilest dishonor, when those evils in which they are involved, react with a dreadful interest on society, then are only they seen, punished and abhorred.

Of the vast number of loose women that infest the streets of this city, a great proportion are so utterly depraved by all manner of low debaucheries, especially by the use of ardent liquors, so totally bereft of shame, that they are, to all appearance, beyond the possibility of reform; whilst others, not yet thus brutalized, nor descended to the lowest sinks of vice, retain a remembrance of their former comparative respectability and comfort, might, by proper means, be restored to a moral course of life, but unfortunately, no such public means exist; the law authorizes but one grade of punishment for common prostitutes, sixty days confinement in Bridewell, which is inadequate to save society from the pestilence of the most depraved class, and demoralizes in a greater degree the other.

It is probable that no public means can be devised to prevent those females throwing themselves in the first instance on the town, which, commonly, is done

in a state of rage and despair, when deserted by their
seducers, and every moral entrance is closed against
them; but even at this point, all is not lost, the moral
principle is not yet extinct, vice aided by despair,
triumphs for the moment, but reflection and remorse
soon succeeds, then should a public asylum receive
the unhappy outcast and complete the work that con-
science has began; but if this moral effort be left un-
aided and to perish, the conclusion is obvious, riot
reigns over a short and wretched existence, and society must take the consequences of its fatal neglect.

There can be no doubt but that great benefit would
result to society from the establishment of a female
penitentiary for the reception of such women as are
not utterly vitiated, and as a means of reforming even
some of those miserable prostitutes that frequently fall
into the hands of the law for petty offences, or are
taken up by the watch, and the following morning
committed to Bridewell: The fate of those women,
however viewed, is truly pitiable, generally seduced,
and abandoned at a tender age, and before their minds
are capable of entertaining ordinary female pride; in
many instances without good parental example—without education, reflection, or fortitude, their characters
blasted, the only resource they see is the brothel, and
when they have received the punishment that the law
prescribes, to the brothel they must return for they
have no other place of shelter. This is not a forced
picture, it is a true description of facts, to the brothel
they must return, or lay in the streets, and in either
event exposed to the savage pranks of midnight ruf-
fians who are as destitute of tenderness or compassion

for the sex under any circumstances, as of common decorum towards each other ; but if a penitentiary asylum was established, it would afford those disposed, a fair opportunity to re-enter society, and the incorrigible would have no excuse left. I, therefore, submit the following project, under a confident opinion of its success, founded on a knowledge of the deplorable and helpless condition of those unfortunate women, and that many of them continue in a state of prostitution unwillingly, having no means of extrication before them.

That a female penitentiary should be established, under the authority of the Mayor and Corporation, in which all the ordinary female work, and trades, shall be carried on, under economical regulations, and a sale store in connection for vending the goods made up. There can be little doubt but that such an institution, would, after the first cost, pay its expenditures, and it is impossible that it should not have a salutary effect, especially if aided by a society of respectable matrons, whose advice and patronage would contribute, in a distinguished manner, to confirm its subjects, in moral and industrious habits.*

————

BROTHEL KEEPERS.

THIS corrupt, and contagious class of persons, whose tartarean depravity spares not even their own

It may be proper to state, that this essay was written, and in press, before the writer had any knowledge that a similar institution was contemplated by a benevolent, and highly respectable association of gentlemen in this city. His source of information was a public advertisement which had he seen earlier, he should have left this branch of his subject with that philanthropic association.

children, seize on the earliest opportunity to ex-
pose them to sale and prostitution, are fit subjects of
the unremitting vengeance of the law, a neighbourhood of them may be truly termed, " hell upon earth."
It is astonishing the address practiced by those bauds
to accomplish the seduction of innocent women
whether married or single, they spare no pains to min-
ister to the palled appetites of their voluptuous custom-
ers, by enticing to their houses, under the mantle of
night, such women of their neighbourhood as circumstances enables them, or their emissaries, to get access
to. The amount of mischief they do in this way, in
what is termed the lower orders of society, is great
and calamitous. The breaking up of families—disper-
sion of children—the ruin of husbands—and the
public prostitution of wives, are often the consequences
of their vile industry, and the detection that commonly ensues.

Our laws and customs admit of no effectual remedy,
for regulating the destructive occupation of those peo-
ple, but the address of a vigorous, and active police,
would go far in deterring them from prowling after
victims yet innocent, and restrict them to the ordinary
sphere of their libidinous calling.

GAMBLING.

THIS vice has got a recommendation from the
higher to the lower classes of society. By those of the
former, who, sometimes, have more money than discretion, practicing it, and with so little regard to the
mandates of the law, that it would seem as if they

were privileged ; but, as nearly all the gambling in this way is done in private houses, amongst select parties, and in confidence, it is difficult, if not impossible, for the law to reach it. But however inaccessible those persons may render themselves, and securely sit down, in their own houses, to impair their fortunes, and injure their families, it is not so with the clubs in the gamb. ling houses, and taverns. These are accessible to the police, and no pains should be spared to uproot them ; in them are to be found sharpers, leading to ruin unsuspecting players, and the habitual idlers, that have dissipated in low excesses, the property left them by industrious parents, morbid in mind and body, have no resource but to lounge out a wretched existence, in such promiscuous company, as the gambling houses, and taverns afford.

Great injury ensues to persons in the middling ranks of life, from the practice of resorting to the billiard tables that are erected, in almost every genteel tavern ; and though gambling, or other dissipation, is never, in the first instance, intended, yet, the consequent loss of valuable time—neglect of business—the wagers for suppers and wine, and the unconquerable habit too often acquired, of daily attending at those places, lead to idleness and dissipation, that in a short time absorb the fruits of many years industry, and end in the ruin of themselves and families.

The fall of persons of this description, is peculiarly grievous and hurtful to society, having in general arisen, by great industry and application, from the poorest class of citizens ; and, if their prosperity was not blasted by temptations, that they have not strength of mind, when involved in, to overcome, would suc.

ceed in establishing their families in affluence and re.
spectability. This delineation is not forced; it is taken
from instances, of which too many may be found in
this city. As the proper authority is armed with power
to stop this great and growing branch of evil, I leave
with them the application, confining myself to a rela.
tion of what has come under my notice.

There is a horde of low gamblers—vagabonds—
agents for passing off counterfeit notes, that prowl
about the suburbs of the city, markets, and wharfs, and
whose standing prey, are seamen and countrymen;
their arts are infinite, and suited to every occasion;
one of which, as it is frequently employed, I shall state.
One of the gang will drop a note close to a person
whom they have previously fixed on to plunder, and
pick it up as having found it; on which another of
them will come up, as if accidentally and a stranger;
when hearing how near the by stander was to the note
when found, (who, commonly, is wishing, and won-
dering, why himself did not see it, and he so near)
promptly gives his opinion that, "this honest man is
entitled by rule to one half." To this the first sharper
seemingly objects, but at length yielding to reason he
generously concludes to "divide what fortune threw
in the way." It is then proposed to get the note (which
is always a counterfeit, lest the person should change
it from his own money on the spot) changed, and
have a drink, to partake of which the man invites the
second sharper who, in his opinion, so generously took
his part. In ten minutes they are all seated in the
back room of some tavern brothel, where they are
joined by the rest of the gang; liquor is brought in,
generally hot, strong toddy, in ten minutes more cards,

or dice are on the table, and, in less than an hour, the simple, and unfortunate poor fellow, is fleeced of his money and watch. It would fill a volume, to relate the address practiced on those occasions. If cunning fails, force is employed, and the plot winds up with the villains running off, leaving the poor wretch unable to follow, either by intoxication or blows. The landlady (a personification of one of the furies) then enters to act her part, loudly declaiming against " the noise made in her house," and demands the reckoning of the sufferer, she soon closes her performance by telling him that " he is a liar and a sharper, and came there, with them other fellows, who ran off, to bilk her house, but if ever he does so again she will send him to bridewell," after which pithy and salutary threat, a bully thrusts him into the street, and the gang re-enter at the back door to divide the spoil, and give the landlady her proportion.

It is very difficult to unkennel a nest of those villains ; the persons they plunder being, generally, nonresidents cannot wait to prosecute them if taken, and the caution they observe renders it very difficult even to commit them, unless as disorderly persons, and when they are indicted, and convicted, it is usually for petit larceny, which involving them but in slight punishment, they are soon at liberty to return to their old pursuits, with keener appetites, and improved caution; there is therefore, no better defence can be had against them than the constant vigilance, and watching of the police agents, annoying them incessantly, and using one of them (when it can be done) against the rest.

TAVERNS. ARDENT LIQUORS.

Probably nothing can demonstrate more strongly the imperfection of even the best constructed governments, than the unlimited licence given to vend, in every street and corner, the most baneful liquor known, the harbinger of ruin to mind and body, of rapine and death, nor can any thing more fully evince the force of habit: thousands will run to see an unfortunate man tied up by the neck against his will, and hang till dead, but no one stops to look at a number of men deliberately committing suicide, by swallowing deadly draughts behind the counter of a grog shop. No doubt, but if one instance was as rare as the other, and that it should be made known that a man was to stand at a certain time and place, and then, and there, publicly swallow a liquid, that should take away his reason, and continue to swallow until it destroyed his nerves, established dropsy and consumption, rotted his intestines, and killed him, there can be little doubt but that the curiosity would be as great, if not greater, to behold so unreasonable and extravagant an exhibition.

Many persons are of opinion, that government is not competent to grapple, successfully, with this formidable hydra, which, if true, would cut the matter short and leave no alternative; but not being under that persuasion, I shall go on to investigate what means are most likely to diminish, if no more, the influence of the most powerful agent of ignorance, depravity, and crime, that the world has any knowledge of.

There have been issued in this city, since the first Tuesday in last May (1811) one thousand seven hun-

dred and forty-one tavern licences, of which about six-
teen hundred are in full operation; and it is expected
that before the first Tuesday in next May, the number
issued, for the twelve months preceding that date, will
exceed two thousand, being in the proportion of one
licence to every forty-seven persons, men women and
children : an instance of public invitation to intemperance, that probably cannot be equalled on the whole
earth; it is no wonder, therefore, that the first judge
of the city and county is on the bench half the year.

The first plan of reform that naturally presents, is to
reduce this almost incredible number, say three-fourths,
and raise the price of licences, say to
dollars, per annum;* this would operate to reduce the
consumption of ardent liquors amongst labouring peo-
ple, particularly with the improvident part of them,
(who are seldom able to purchase more than a gill, or
half a pint at a time) by raising the price, and reducing the number of sellers; at present, a woman of this
class of rum drinkers, does not hesitate to lay her in-
fant on the floor and run, barefooted, and bareheaded,
with a broken teapot, or pitcher in her hand, " just to
the next corner for a gill of rum ;" but if this fascinat-
ing shop was removed a mile, or half a mile, from her,
the visit would be less frequent, consequently there
would be less consumption of liquor by this woman,
and some degree of reformation must ensue : Look at
two or three men, of the same character, met together
at a corner; it is impossible that they should turn

* Prejudices will, most likely, be excited against the writer, for the
promulgation of these opinions; but whilst he regrets that such a consequence should ensue, he ought not, therefore, to yield a right, nor decline
a duty; those respectable dealers in spirituous liquors, who disapprove of
the abuses of its use, will not, he is confident, permit their opinions to be
influenced by misrepresentations.

round without seeing a tavern or a grog shop; no consequence was ever more certain; to it they must go, and there spend every cent they have, whatever may be the distress of their families; but if this temptation was not before them, steaming forth the enchanting odour of a liquor cask, which they inhale with as keen a zest as ever stimulated a glutton or epicure, they would often separate without drinking, and carry home the money, that otherwise is left in the till of a grog shop. Certainly an arrangement that should reduce, even one half of the present excitement and intemperance, would so far be beneficial; and if no more effectual remedy can be had, that itself would be of great importance; but a more general corrective is necessary, and is attainable, which simply is, to render ardent liquors too dear for any class of society to use, except as a medicine. This can only be done by laying high duties on foreign and domestic spirits; for if they are permitted to be brought out of the ship or distillery cheap, no laws can prevent their being retailed cheap.

Permanent and effectual restrictions on the consumption of ardent liquors, would operate as a bounty on brewing, and our cities and towns would soon abound with an eligible substitute, the fine ale, that already is supposed to be equal to any in the world, and, under such circumstances of encouragement, could be retailed at three cents a pint, which is the lowest grog shop price, for a gill of poison, under the name of spirits, and which quantity is taken at one draught by an ordinary grog drinker.

A relish for ardent liquor, in a man or woman of low circumstances, commonly terminates in drunkenness and premature death; and even among that class that have all the advantages of good example, education and fortune, how few there are that have strength of mind to emancipate themselves from this intemperance, when once it fastens on them. It approaches them under the mask of good fellowship, and at length settles down in solitary inebriation; but with those, the consequences, though calamitous, are not often fatal in the extreme, some branch of the family saves the offspring from distress, but it is not so with the poor; with them utter ruin follows; for the truth of which, I refer to a view of the brothels, and to an examination of the persons confined in our state and city prisons.

I close this branch of the subject, with an opinion founded on due examination and reflection, THAT UP-WARDS OF THREE HUNDRED PERSONS, MEN AND WOMEN, PERISH ANNUALLY IN THIS CITY, WHOSE DEATHS ARE OCCASIONED, DIRECTLY OR INDIRECTLY, BY THE EXCESSIVE USE OF ARDENT LIQUORS.*

PAWNBROKERS, DEALERS IN OLD CLOTHES, AND DEALERS IN JUNK AND SHIP IRON.

THE great accommodation that pawn broker's shops, old clothes, and junk stands, afford to petty felons in putting off their plunder promptly, and without being troubled with questions, points them out as proper objects of police regulation. No doubt but there are some honest and well disposed persons in those

---

* The writer purposes taking up this subject, with other branches of civil police, more fully, and to exhibit the operation of our inferior courts of law, denominated ward courts, on society in general, and on the ignorant poor in particular.

callings, that would not receive goods, knowing, or suspecting them to be stolen; but that there are some of a different character, particularly of the old clothes and junk fraternity, I am well assured. If those occupations are necessary for the accommodation of a part of society, it is no less necessary, for the interest of the whole, that they should be licenced, and the greatest care taken that none are licenced but persons of good character, and that their stores and recesses, shall be accessible to the agents of the police, by order of a magistrate. That this, or some other system of regulation for those occupations, (which are rapidly spreading over the city, and conducted, in most instances, by persons little known, and without responsibility of character) has become necessary, the records of the courts of general sessions of the peace, will fully establish.

INTELLIGENCE OFFICES.

THIS occupation is so intimately connected with the safety of families, and especially with the morals of so many poor and friendless females (this allusion may be sufficient on this point) that probably, it should be assumed by the public, and made a branch of police duty, which may be done with greater advantages to all parties concerned, than any private institution of the kind can possibly afford. To accomplish this, it is necessary that a law should be enacted, directing that a general intelligence office for servants shall be opened under the superintendance of the police; the register of which, should connect and exhibit at one view, and for one cost, all the applications of masters and servants within the city; this alone would be a great accommodation and such as no private office can ever afford; but as a means of preserving the morals of domestics, it would be invaluable; the circumstance of being known and recommended by the police, would tend to correct their excesses, and, in the worst event, would facilitate the arrest of such of them, as should abuse the confidence reposed in their honesty by their employers. The great benefits that would arise to the public from this system, to masters, and honest, sober servants (to whom it would be a special protection) will readily be seen by all heads of families, particularly by gentlemen conversant in public business.

GENERAL OBSERVATIONS.

ON reviewing the great variety of character making up the population of a large city; the obvious inequalities of fortune; the insatiable appetite for animal gratification, at any sacrifice, in weak and depraved minds; the boisterous passions of some; the timidity of others, and the wiles of those peculiarly dangerous characters, that are forever on the watch to take advantage of the folly or misfortune of others, when these and the many other traits in the human character, are considered, it is no longer a matter of wonder, that so much wretchedness exists, in such a heterogeneous mass.

It is more difficult to establish an efficient system of preventive police, and the prevention of crimes is its essence, under a free, than under an arbitary government, for the laws that guards the rights and liberty of an honest man, are applicable in their forms, to the vicious that live in a constant state of open or, secret hostility against both. Much has been said of the great perfection of the police of certain nations, but those eulogists do not advert to the fact, that its agents are restricted by no laws, nor power, but the will of one man, that they can enter, without previous form of law, by day or night, any man's dwelling, ransack it over, and retire without informing him the object of their visit, and happy is he, if the insult and alarm are all that he suffers, but may our good genius forever preserve us from such perfection and power of police as this; which can only accompany despotism, and is the hateful attribute of fearful tyrants.

The legal forms that, with us, prevent the prompt developement and defeat of criminal plans, may be balanced by constant vigilance, a judicious application of the authority which may be vested, skilful address, and a competent knowledge of the human character in all grades of life. Much also depends on the local residence of the police authority. The suburbs of this city are annoyed, in a much greater degree than the centre, by the brutal effusions of vulgar and intemperate persons, common disturbers of the peace, and is, almost, exclusively the retreat of sharpers, passers of counterfeit money, pick-pockets, and other villains, that have their dens in those parts of the town. It would be a great advantage to the public in general, and manifestly so to the citizens residing in the upper parts of the city, if the police office was established in that quarter; say at the watch house, at the head of Chatham-street; for those that have no respect for society, or the laws, fear their agents; and on this fact I premise the opinion, that the establishment of the police office in the neighbourhood of such persons, would have an excellent effect to disconcert their schemes, root them out of their lurking holes, and render the situation of the citizens more secure. Where danger is greatest, there should the sentry be placed, and the police should be the Cerberus of society, guarding from danger every man's door, protecting from oppression the innocent and helpless, and formidable to the vicious, whom they should watch, follow, and disconcert, without ceasing.

PUBLIC BATHS.

I CANNOT omit remarking (though the subject is not connected with criminal police, it appertains to the general system of regulation and good order) that it would be highly convenient and beneficial to the public, generally, if the Corporation were to establish public baths for the use of the citizens. In several diseases, bathing is thought essential to the restoration of health; but the price of private baths is so great, (thirty-seven and a half cents each, in summer, and fifty cents in winter) that none but persons in easy circumstances can afford to use them; poor citizens are, therefore, shut out from this auxiliary to health, and necessary accommodation.

The public may afford, cold, warm, and steam baths, in all seasons, for, or less than twelve and a half cents each; but one superintendent would be necessary, assisted by attendants selected from the alms house, whose services at the baths would involve no additional expence.

If baths were established at a moderate price, the use of them would soon become general, and thus an excellent custom would be introduced, tending to cleanliness, good order, and health.

> " This is the purest exercise of health,
> " The kind refresher of the summer heats."

It is clearly within the province of the corporation to erect public baths. They are necessary, in many instances, to health. They are especially necessary in summer to cleanliness and comfort. They are so expensive that none but wealthy citizens can afford to have them erected in their houses. It is therefore, it would seem, incumbent on the government to supply the deficiency, and see that no class of citizens suffers for want of a necessary accommodation, when it can so easily, and without expense, be furnished by the public. It may be further observed, that public baths was a branch of the police of the ancient republics, and that the citizens were not only accommodated by the government, but splendidly served with this means of public and private decorum. The magnificent remains of Grecian and Roman baths, evince the great care, and immense sums expended on that object.

The establishment of public baths would prevent the exhibition of nakedness, and the annoyance of female modesty exhibited on the margin of our rivers, and against which our common council have legislated in vain.

There can be no doubt but that bodily cleanliness has a favourable effect on moral purity. Thomson has well said,

> " E'en from the body's purity, the mind
> " Receives a secret sympathetic aid."

In this summary of the police of this city, I might have adduced numerous facts in corroboration oi the opinions given; but as that might have the appearance of a desire to excite curiosity, or to torture the feelings of individuals, I have declined it, nor is it my intention to point at the weakness or vice of persons in particular; such motives are not within my view; but to contribute my humble efforts to the good order and security of society,, and to ameliorate, if possible, the condition of those improvident persons, who, unable to withstand the temptations before them, dissipate, to the ruin of themselves and families, the scanty wages of labour.

THE END.

APPENDIX.

THE writer has seen, with great satisfaction, that his opinions on the Police of this city, correspond with those delivered by his Honor the Mayor, in his charge to the Grand Jury, last December session. He has read with much advantage, the luminous charges of that able magistrate, who is best qualified, from his situation, to form correct opinions on that subject; but it may not be irrelative to add, that this essay on the Police, was in the press at the time the above mentioned charge was delivered.